JP-Dahl

123 sticker

**Know Your Numbers**

# Eggs and Legs

## Counting by Twos

by Michael Dahl        illustrated by Todd Ouren

Special thanks to our advisers for their expertise:

Stuart Farm, M.Ed., Mathematics Lecturer
University of North Dakota, Grand Forks

Susan Kesselring, M.A., Literacy Educator
Rosemount-Apple Valley-Eagan (Minnesota) School District

PICTURE WINDOW BOOKS
Minneapolis, Minnesota

Managing Editor: Catherine Neitge
Creative Director: Terri Foley
Art Director: Keith Griffin
Editor: Christianne Jones
Designer: Todd Ouren
Page production: Picture Window Books
The illustrations in this book were prepared digitally.

Picture Window Books
1710 Roe Crest Drive
North Mankato, MN 56003
www.capstonepub.com

 All books published by Picture Window Books are manufactured with paper containing at least 10 percent post-consumer waste.

Library of Congress Cataloging-in-Publication Data
Dahl, Michael.
Eggs and legs : counting by twos / written by Michael Dahl; illustrated by Todd Ouren.
p. cm. — (Know your numbers)
ISBN 978-1-4048-0945-1 (hardcover)
ISBN 978-1-4048-1114-0 (paperback)
1. Counting—Juvenile literature. 2. Multiplication—Juvenile literature. I. Ouren, Todd, ill. II. Title.

QA113.D328 2005
513.2'11—dc22                       2004019004

Printed in the United States of America in North Mankato, Minnesota.
032012      006670R

Mrs. Hen stared at her empty nest.

TWO little legs went running into the barn.

FOUR little legs were hiding in the corn.

SIX little legs were chasing the dog.

8

9

EIGHT little legs were
bothering a cow.

10

12

TEN little legs were climbing
on the tractor.

TWELVE little legs were playing with the pig.

15

FOURTEEN little legs were scurrying through the beans.

2 4 6 8 10 12 14

16

SIXTEEN little legs were
scaring the geese.

2 4 6 8 10 12 14 16

18

19

EIGHTEEN little legs were scooped up by the farmer's wife.

TWENTY little legs were back in the nest.

:2 :4 :6 :8 :10 :12 :14 :16 :18 :20

22

"Whew!" said Mrs. Hen. "These chicks really keep me on my toes!"

## Fun Facts

- A hen lays an average of 300 eggs a year.
- A mother hen turns over her eggs about 50 times a day.
- The biggest chicken egg weighed more than 1 pound (.45 kilograms).
- Most chicken eggs are either white or brown, but some chickens lay blue-green eggs.
- There are more chickens in the world than people.
- The record number of yolks found in a single egg is nine.

## On the Web

FactHound offers a safe, fun way to find Web sites related to topics in this book. All of the sites on FactHound have been researched by our staff.

1. Visit www.facthound.com
2. Type in this special code: 1404809457
3. Click on the FETCH IT button.

Your trusty FactHound will fetch the best Web sites for you!

## Find the Numbers

Now you have finished reading the story, but a surprise still awaits you. Hidden in each picture is a multiple of 2 from 2 to 20. Can you find them all?

**2**–the hook above the door

**4**–the handle of the shovel

**6**–on the wheelbarrow wheel

**8**–the pulley on the well

**10**–on the tractor engine

**12**–on the mud splash on the right page

**14**–above the beans on the right page

**16**–between the wings of the goose

**18**–between the four eggs on the left

**20**–on the bottom right eggshell

## Look for all of the books in the Know Your Numbers series: